St. Jude Devotions, Novenas and Prayer Book

Friends of St. Jude

Edited by Jeanette Roberts, M. A.

Bloomingdale Press, Bloomingdale, Ohio

DEDICATION

To all those in need of God's help, especially those in desperate circumstances.

" But you, my beloved, building yourselves upon your most holy faith, praying in the Holy Ghost, keep yourselves in the love of God, waiting for the mercy of our Lord Jesus Christ, unto life everlasting."(Jude 1: 20-21)

Table of Contents

S. JUDE.

A Dieu seul nôtre Sauveur, par nôtre Seigneur Jesus-Christ, gloire et magnifi-
cence, empire, et force. S. Jude, v. 25

https://www.metmuseum.org/art/collection/search/394032
Artist: Etienne Brion (French, Paris, ca.1700), Date: 1726
Medium: Etching and engraving
Credit Line: The Elisha Whittelsey Collection, The Elisha Whittelsey Fund, 1959
Accession Number: 59.570.448(13)

INTRODUCTION

The power of consistent prayer is immense. The all-knowing God has an infinite and personal love for every individual human being. Through the example and words of His Son Jesus Christ, mankind has been taught that prayer is pleasing to God and necessary for salvation. Jesus Christ instructs us to pray always, to pray daily, to watch and pray, to pray in secret, to pray in groups, to ask God insistently and urgently for help. God hears the prayers of all who call upon Him from their hearts. A soul may see results of prayer immediately or may never see results in this life. But God, who has numbered all the hairs of your head, hears prayers and will answer those who call upon Him. Through their meritorious lives, the saints in Heaven are close to God and intercede for mankind, especially when called upon to do so, just as true friends are always there when help is needed. On earth, we see spiritual matters dimly, and in a material way, as through a dark glass, but the saints have deeper understanding and love of God, because they see Him face to face. They bring our prayers like incense before Him.

Why St. Jude?

St. Jude is considered the patron saint of desperate or hopeless cases because in his letter (which is found right before the Book of the Apocalypse in the New Testament) he encourages his readers to have hope and to pray in the Holy Spirit despite the hopeless and Godless times in which they were living. He describes the bleak and desperate times in his letter. Church tradition has regarded St. Jude as the patron of impossible causes for centuries. His feast day is October 28.

A novena is a nine day prayer or prayers said for a particular intention. Nine days are symbolic of the 9 days between the Ascension of Jesus into heaven and the descent of the Holy Spirit on Pentecost, when the Apostles prayed together in an upper room. As mentioned above, the Feast Day of St. Jude is October 28 though these novenas may be said at any time.

1 NOVENA PRAYER TO ST. JUDE PATRON OF IMPOSSIBLE CAUSES

Powerful novena prayer to be said for nine consecutive days

O most holy apostle, Saint Jude, faithful servant and friend of Jesus, the Church honors and invokes you universally, as the patron of hopeless cases, and of things almost despaired of. Pray for me, who am so miserable. Make use, I implore you, of that particular privilege accorded to you, to bring visible and speedy help where help was almost despaired of. Come to my assistance in this great need, that I may receive the consolation and help of Heaven in all my necessities, tribulations, and sufferings, particularly (here make your request) and that I may praise God with you and all the elect throughout eternity. I promise you, O blessed Jude, to be ever mindful of this great favor, to always honor you as my special and powerful patron, and to gratefully encourage devotion to you. Amen.

For centuries, St. Jude, (sometimes referred to in the Bible as "Thaddeus") not to be confused with Judas, who betrayed Christ, is called upon in hopeless or desperate situations because in his letter in Sacred Scripture he urges followers of Christ to persevere, as their ancestors had done, in difficult circumstances. It is said that after St. Jude was martyred, many people came to pray at his grave and received answers and blessings for their prayers, many of them said in desperation. St. Bernard and also St. Bridget of Sweden reported that God wants us to call St. Jude the saint for the hopeless and for things despaired of. Many healings and miracles have been associated with this prayer.

+++

Novena to St. Jude for those suffering great personal affliction

S T. JUDE THADDEUS, relative of Jesus and Mary, glorious Apostle and Martyr renowned for thy virtues and miracles, faithful and prompt intercessor for all who honor thee and trust in thee, powerful patron and helper in grievous affliction, I come to thee and entreat thee with all my heart to come to my aid, for thou hast received from God the privilege of assisting with manifest help those who almost despair! Look down upon me: my life is a life of crosses, my days are full of tribulation and my paths are strewn with thorns---and scarcely one moment passes but is witness of my tears and sighs. My soul is enveloped in darkness, disquietude, discouragement, mistrust---yes, sometimes even a kind of despair preys upon me. Divine Providence seems lost to my sight, and faith seems to falter in my heart. Overwhelmed by these thoughts, I see myself surrounded by a dark cloud. Thou canst not forsake me in this sad plight! I will not depart from thee until thou hast heard me. Oh, hasten to my aid! I will thank God for the graces bestowed upon thee, and will propagate thine honor according to my power. Amen.

Note: Many have been helped by saying this popular and highly efficacious novena.

2 PRAYER FOR THE SICK THROUGH THE INTERCESSION OF ST. JUDE

Prayer for the sick

St. Jude, you witnessed the healing power of our Lord Jesus. You saw his compassion for the sick and dying. You yourself touched the sick, shared the sorrows of the mournful, and encouraged the despairing. You received this authority and healing power to work wonders, to cure the incurable, to make people whole. We ask you to intercede with our brother, Jesus, to send his saving grace to heal the sickness and suffering of (name the person who is sick) to uplift his/her despondent spirits, and to instill hope in his/her heart. Amen.

Say this prayer daily for the sick person. Have faith that St. Jude will carry your prayer to God.

+++

Prayers for patients in critical condition

Dear Apostle and Martyr for Christ, you left us an Epistle in the New Testament. With good reason many invoke you when illness is at a desperate stage. We now recommend to your kindness (name of patient) who is in a critical condition. May the cure of this patient increase his/her faith and love for the Lord of Life, for the glory of our merciful God. Amen.

+++

St. Jude, you remained faithful to our Lord, even unto death. You gave your life so that others might live. You endured physical pain and emotional abandonment. But you gladly joined your sufferings to those of our Savior, Jesus, and thus shared in the redemption of the world. I ask you now to intercede with our brother, Jesus Christ on my behalf, so that I too can find strength in the face of my suffering. Help me to trust in God and put my life in his hands. Amen

Some people ask why we ask St. Jude to intercede with God, rather than go directly to Jesus with our problems. St. Thomas Aquinas addresses this question in the Summa Theologica II:II, question 83, article 11, where he says:

> ...since prayers offered for others proceed from charity,. . . , the greater the charity of the saints in heaven, the more they pray for wayfarers, since the latter can be helped by prayers: and the more closely they are united to God, the more are their prayers efficacious: for the Divine order is such that lower beings receive an overflow of the excellence of the higher, even as the air receives the brightness of the sun. Wherefore it is said of Christ (Hebrews 7:25): "Going to God by His own power . . . to make intercession for us" [Vulgate: 'He is able to save for ever them that come to God by Him, always living to make intercession for us.'] Hence Jerome says (Cont. Vigilant. 6): "If the apostles and martyrs while yet in the body and having to be solicitous for themselves, can pray for others, how much more now that they have the crown of victory and triumph." (Summa Theologica II-II: 83: 11)

NOTE: Many miracles and unexpected healings have been reported through the intercession of St. Jude. It is worthwhile to ask St. Jude to pray for the sick, even for those in terminal or critical stages. Sometimes God chooses to heal these patients, or He may choose to prepare them and those who love them for the Eternity toward which each of us travels.

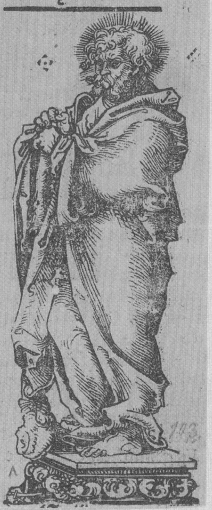

S. Judas Thadeus.

jtzt trage/habe vnd
rblich ist/ am Jüng/
n tag werd wider/
ib erweckt durch
ottes stimme / wie
Christus zuuor er/
nden ist von tod/
t.

Die Aufferstehung
r Todten / ist ein
os geheimnis der
öttlichen Maiestet/
elches Menschliche
rnunfft nicht kan
rstehen / vnd sol es
ch nicht wissen/son/
rn allein gleuben.
enn eben der leib/
mit jtzt mein See/
sündigt/ oder fastet
d guts wircket /
ird am Jüngsten
ge wider erweckt/
d mit meiner Seele

3 LONGER NOVENA TO ST. JUDE

First Day

Most holy St. Jude – apostle, martyr and friend of Jesus, today I ask that you pray for me and my intentions:

(mention your intentions here)

You are the patron of the impossible. Pray for me and my intentions. O St. Jude, pray that God's grace and mercy will cover my intentions. Pray for the impossible if it is God's will.

Pray that I may have the grace to accept God's holy will even if it is painful and difficult for me.

St. Jude, you loved our Lord, help me to love Him more.

O St. Jude, pray for me that I may grow in faith, hope and love and in the grace of Jesus Christ. Pray for these intentions, but most of all pray that I may join you in heaven with God for all eternity. Amen.

Day 2 – St. Jude Novena

Most holy St. Jude – apostle, martyr and friend of Jesus, today I ask that you pray for me and my intentions!

(State your intentions here)

You are the patron of the impossible. Pray for me and my intentions! O St. Jude pray that God's grace and mercy will cover my intentions. Pray for the impossible if it is God's will.

Pray that I may have the grace to accept God's holy will even if it is painful and difficult for me.

St. Jude, pray that I may have your zeal to preach the Gospel.

O St. Jude, pray for me that I may grow in faith, hope and love and in the grace of Jesus Christ. Pray for these intentions, but most of all pray that I may join you in heaven with God for all eternity. Amen.

Day 3 – St. Jude Novena

Most holy St. Jude – apostle, martyr and friend of Jesus, today I ask that you pray for me and my intentions!

(State your intentions here)

You are the patron of the impossible. Pray for me and my intentions! O St. Jude, pray that God's grace and mercy will cover my intentions. Pray for the impossible if it is God's will.

Pray that I may have the grace to accept God's holy will even if it is painful and difficult for me.

St. Jude, you labored for years, pray that I may have patience in my struggles.

O St. Jude, pray for me that I may grow in faith, hope and love and in the grace of Jesus Christ. Pray for these intentions, but most of all pray that I may join you in heaven with God for all eternity. Amen.

Day 4 – St. Jude Novena

Most holy St. Jude – apostle, martyr and friend of Jesus, today I ask that you pray for me and my intentions!

(State your intentions here)

You are the patron of the impossible. Pray for me and my intentions! O St. Jude, pray that God's grace and mercy will cover my intentions. Pray for the impossible if it is God's will.

Pray that I may have the grace to accept God's holy will even if it is painful and difficult for me.

St. Jude, you are known for answering lost causes, pray for my most impossible needs.

O St. Jude, pray for me that I may grow in faith, hope and love and in the grace of Jesus Christ. Pray for these intentions, but most of all pray that I may join you in heaven with God for all eternity. Amen.

Day 5 – St. Jude Novena

Most holy St. Jude – apostle, martyr and friend of Jesus, today I ask that you pray for me and my intentions!

(State your intentions here)

You are the patron of the impossible. Pray for me and my intentions! O St. Jude, pray that God's grace and mercy will cover my intentions. Pray for the impossible if it is God's will.

Pray that I may have the grace to accept God's holy will even if it is painful and difficult for me.

St. Jude, you sacrificed for the Kingdom of God, pray that I may sacrifice like you.

O St. Jude, pray for me that I may grow in faith, hope and love and in the grace of Jesus Christ. Pray for these intentions, but most of all pray that I may join you in heaven with God for all eternity. Amen.

Day 6 – St. Jude Novena

Most holy St. Jude – apostle, martyr and friend of Jesus, today I ask that you pray for me and my intentions!

(State your intentions here)

You are the patron of the impossible. Pray for me and my intentions! O St. Jude, pray that God's grace and mercy will cover my intentions. Pray for the impossible if it is God's will.

Pray that I may have the grace to accept God's holy will even if it is painful and difficult for me.

St. Jude, pray that I may know God's will in my life.

O St. Jude, pray for me that I may grow in faith, hope and love and in the grace of Jesus Christ. Pray for these intentions, but most of all pray that I may join you in heaven with God for all eternity. Amen.

Day 7 – St. Jude Novena

Most holy St. Jude – apostle, martyr and friend of Jesus, today I ask that you pray for me and my intentions!

(State your intentions here)

You are the patron of the impossible. Pray for me and my intentions! O St. Jude, pray that God's grace and mercy will cover my intentions. Pray for the impossible if it is God's will.

Pray that I may have the grace to accept God's holy will even if it is painful and difficult for me.

St. Jude, pray that I may put my trust in God that He knows my needs even better than I do and that He provides.

O St. Jude, pray for me that I may grow in faith, hope and love and in the grace of Jesus Christ. Pray for these intentions, but most of all pray that I may join you in heaven with God for all eternity. Amen.

Day 8 – St. Jude Novena

Most holy St. Jude – apostle, martyr and friend of Jesus, today I ask that you pray for me and my intentions!

(State your intentions here)

You are the patron of the impossible. Pray for me and my intentions! O St. Jude, pray that God's grace and mercy will cover my intentions. Pray for the impossible if it is God's will.

Pray that I may have the grace to accept God's holy will even if it is painful and difficult for me.

St. Jude, pray for me that I will not lose hope.

O St. Jude, pray for me that I may grow in faith, hope and love and in the grace of Jesus Christ. Pray for these intentions, but most of all pray that I may join you in heaven with God for all eternity. Amen.

Day 9 – St. Jude Novena

Most holy St. Jude – apostle, martyr and friend of Jesus, today I ask that you pray for me and my intentions!

(State your intentions here)

You are the patron of the impossible. Pray for me and my intentions! O St. Jude, pray that God's grace and mercy will cover my intentions. Pray for the impossible if it is God's will.

Pray that I may have the grace to accept God's holy will even if it is painful and difficult for me.

St. Jude, pray for me that I will not lose faith.

O St. Jude, pray for me that I may grow in faith, hope and love and in the grace of Jesus Christ. Pray for these intentions, but most of all pray that I may join you in heaven with God for all eternity. Amen.

+++

Judas

XI.

CARNIS RESVRRECTIONEM.

Series/Portfolio: Christ and the Apostles
Artist: Hendrick Goltzius (Netherlandish, Mühlbracht 1558–1617 Haarlem)
Date: ca. 1589 , Medium: Engraving
Credit Line: Bequest of Phyllis Massar, 2011
Accession Number: 2012.136.471.12

4 MORE NOVENAS TO ST. JUDE

St. Jude, through prayer you praised God for the wonderful works of Jesus. You asked God for the strength to meet the challenges of your apostolate. You put your trust in God's mercy, believing firmly that God loved you and understood your joys and sorrows, your hopes and fears, and your triumphs and failures. You understood that nothing is impossible for God. I ask you to pray for me now before the Most High so that I too might be filled with God's saving power, understand God's will for me and faithfully place myself in God's loving hands.

+++

h glorious apostle St. Jude, faithful servant and friend of Jesus, the name of the traitor who delivered thy beloved Master into the hands of His enemies has caused thee to be forgotten by many, but the Church honors and invokes thee universally as the patron of hopeless cases--of things despaired of. Pray for me who am so miserable; make use, I implore thee, of that particular privilege accorded thee of bringing visible and speedy help where help is almost despaired of. Come to my assistance in this great need, that I may receive the consolations and succor of heaven in all my necessities, tribulations and sufferings, particularly (mention your request), and that I may bless God with thee and all the elect throughout eternity. I promise thee, O blessed St. Jude, to be ever mindful of this great favor, and I will never cease to honor thee as my special and powerful patron, and to do all in my power to encourage devotion to thee. Amen

+++

Novena to Saint Jude (Nine consecutive days)

O Holy St Jude! Apostle and Martyr, great in virtue and rich in miracles, near kinsman of Jesus Christ, faithful intercessor for all who invoke you, special patron in time of need; to you I have recourse from the depth of my heart, and humbly beg you, to whom God has given such great power, to come to my assistance; help me now in my urgent need and grant my earnest petition. I will never forget thy graces and favors you obtain for me and I will do my utmost to spread devotion to you. Amen.

5 SHORT PRAYERS AND INVOCATIONS TO ST. JUDE

"May the Sacred Heart of Jesus be adored, glorified, loved and preserved now and forever. Sacred Heart of Jesus have mercy on us, Saint Jude worker of Miracles, pray for us, Saint Jude helper and keeper of the hopeless, pray for us, Thank you Saint Jude."

+++

St. Jude, pray for us and all who honor thee and invoke thy aid.
(Say 3 Our Father's, 3 Hail Mary's, and 3 Glory Be's after this.)

+++

Another short novena:

O Holy St. Jude! Apostle and Martyr, great in virtue and rich in miracles, near kinsman of Jesus Christ, faithful intercessor for all who invoke you, special patron in time of need, to you I have recourse from the depth of my heart, and humbly beg you, to whom God has given such great power, to come to my assistance; help me now in my urgent need and grant my earnest petition. I will never forget thy graces and favors you obtain for me and I will do my utmost to spread devotion to you. Amen.

+++

St. Jude, pray for me!

15

+++

St. Jude, ask Jesus to cure me!

+++

St. Jude, be my advocate with God the Father, God the Son and God the Holy Spirit, Amen!

+++

St. Jude, make haste to help me in my hour of need! Amen.

6 WHO IS ST. JUDE?

The Catholic Encyclopedia (1913 Edition) identifies St. Jude as one of the twelve apostles of Jesus, referred to as "Thaddeus". It has this to say about St. Jude:

"(1) Jude in the Books of the New Testament

In the address of the Epistle the author styles himself "Jude, the servant of Jesus Christ and brother of James". "Servant of Jesus Christ" means "apostolic minister or labourer". "Brother of James" denotes him as the brother of James (kat exochen) who was well-known to the Hebrew Christians to whom the Epistle of St. Jude was written. This James is to be identified with the Bishop of the Church of Jerusalem (Acts, xv, 13; xxi, 18), spoken of by St. Paul as "the brother of the Lord" (Gal. i, 19), who was the author of the Catholic Epistle of St. James and is regarded amongst Catholic interpreters as the Apostle James the son of Alpheus (St. James the Less). This last identification, however, is not evident, nor, from a critical point of view, does it seem beyond all doubt. Most Catholic commentators identify Jude with the "Judas Jacobi" ("Jude, the brother of James" in the D.V.) of Luke, vi, 16, and Acts, i, 13 — also called Thaddeus Matt. x, 3: Mark, iii, 18) — referring the expression to the fact that his brother James was better known than himself in the primitive Church. This view is strongly confirmed by the title "the brother of James", by which Jude designates himself in the address of

17

his Epistle. If this identification is proved, it is clear that Jude, the author of the Epistle, was reckoned among the Twelve Apostles. This opinion is most highly probable. Beyond this we find no further information concerning Jude in the New Testament, except that the "brethren of the Lord", among whom Jude was included, were known to the Galatians and the Corinthians; also that several of them were married, and that they did not fully believe in Christ till after the Resurrection (I Cor., ix, 5; Gal., i, 10; John, vii, 3-5; Acts, i, 14). From a fact of Hegesippus told by Eusebius (Hist. eccl., III, xix, xx, xxii) we learn that Jude was "said to have been the brother of the Lord according to the flesh", and that two of his grandsons lived till the reign of Trajan."

7 WHO IS ST. JUDE? REFERENCES FROM SACRED SCRIPTURE

We have evidence of the existence of St. Jude in the writings of Sacred Scripture. St. Jude is spoken of by all four Gospel writers, and in the Acts of the Apostles. St. Jude's own epistle, placed directly before the Book of Revelation, testifies to his life among us. The following are the Biblical passages that reference St. Jude:

St. Matthew and St. Mark

55 "Is not this the carpenter's son? Is not his mother called Mary, and his brethren James, and Joseph, and Simon, and Jude (Mt. 13:55)", and also in the Gospel of St. Mark: 3 "Is not this the carpenter, the son of Mary, the brother of James, and Joseph, and Jude, and Simon? Are not also his sisters here with us? And they were scandalized in regard of him." (Mk. 6:3)

St. Jude is identified as "Thaddeus" in the Gospels of St. Matthew and St. Mark:

10 And having called his twelve disciples together, he gave them power over unclean spirits, to cast them out, and to heal all manner of diseases, and all manner of infirmities.

2 And the names of the twelve apostles are these: The first, Simon who is called Peter, and Andrew his brother,3 James the son of Zebedee, and John his brother, Philip and Bartholomew, Thomas and Matthew the publican, and James the son of Alpheus and Thaddeus, 4 Simon the Cananean, and Judas Iscariot, who also betrayed him."(Mt.10:1-4)

St. Mark

17 And James the son of Zebedee, and John the brother of James; and he named them Boanerges, which is, The sons of thunder: 18 And Andrew and Philip, and Bartholomew and Matthew, and Thomas and James of Alpheus, and Thaddeus, and Simon the Cananean: 19 And Judas Iscariot, who also betrayed him. (Mk. 3:17-19)

St. Luke

In St. Luke, Chapter 6, he enumerates the twelve disciples of Jesus "Jude the brother of James, and Judas Iscariot, who turned traitor." (Lk 6:16)

St. John

Gospel of St. John: "Judas saith to him, not the Iscariot: Lord, how is it, that thou wilt manifest thyself to us, and not to the world? 23 Jesus answered, and said to him: If any one love me, he will keep my word, and my Father will love him, and we will come to him, and will make our abode with him." (Jn 14:22-23)

Acts of the Apostles

Again, St. Jude is mentioned in the Acts of the Apostles: "And when they were come in, they went up into an upper room, where abode Peter and John, James and Andrew Philip and Thomas, Bartholomew and Matthew, James of Alpheus, and Simon Zelotes and Jude the brother of James. All these were persevering with one mind in prayer with the women, and Mary the mother of Jesus, and with his brethren."(Acts 1:13-14)

Epistle of St. Jude

Finally, the Epistle of St. Jude, in Catholic Bibles, is found after the Third Epistle of St. John, and directly before the Apocalypse (Revelation) of St. John in the New Testament. It was written between the years 62-67 AD, after the death of St. James, but before the death of St. Peter.

8 WHO IS ST. JUDE?   SACRED TRADITION

As mentioned, St. Jude Thaddeus, one of the Twelve Apostles, identifies himself in his letter saying "Jude, the servant of Jesus Christ and brother of James" (Jude, 1:1), meaning that he working as a laborer for Christ, and that being James's brother, he is related by blood to Jesus, Mary and Joseph.

When the Holy Spirit descended upon the Apostles and Mary, St. Jude, along with the others received the gifts, but we don't hear anything about his life's work in the Scriptures. Stories from Church tradition tell us that he spread the Good News of Jesus Christ throughout Judea, Syria, Beirut, Samaria (Palestine), Idumaea and Mesopotamia (Edessa). He was a fellow laborer with St. Simon and they were both martyred by being clubbed to death in Suanir, in Persia (Iran).

St. Bridget of Sweden, a twelfth century saint, and St. Bernard of Clairvaux in France had visions from God telling them to pray through the intercession of St. Jude as The Patron Saint of the Impossible', as he would be most willing to help.

Church tradition has long designated St. Jude as the saint of impossible causes, and to whom we should turn when all hope is lost.

After he died by martyrdom, St. Jude's body was brought to Rome and placed in a crypt in St. Peter's Basilica. His bones currently reside in the left transept of the Basilica under the main altar of St. Joseph. He shares a tomb with the Apostle Simon Zealot, who died with him.

g) St. Thaddeus, St. Sandukht and other Christians in Sanatruk's prison, Armenian History in Italian Art - Հայոց
Պատմության Էջեր
   17:57, 14 December 2009 (UTC)
   Fusaro (19th cent.)

9 TRADITIONAL IMAGES AND ICONS OF ST. JUDE

St. Jude with Flame

You have probably seen images or statues of St. Jude with a flame over his head. This reminds us of St. Jude's presence on the day of Pentecost—when the Holy Spirit descended upon the Apostles and Mary and filled them with His gifts. It is described thus in the Acts of the Apostles:

"When the day of Pentecost came, they were all together in one place. Suddenly a sound like the blowing of a violent wind came from heaven and filled the whole house where they were sitting. 3 They saw what seemed to be tongues of fire that separated and came to rest on each of them. 4 All of them were filled with the Holy Spirit and began to speak in other tongues[a] as the Spirit enabled them." (Act 2: 1-4)

St. Jude Holding Medallion

Another popular representation of St. Jude is that of him holding a medallion with an image of Jesus Christ. This tradition came from an account by the ancient historian Eusebius who reported that the Apostle Thomas sent St. Jude to King Agbar of Edessa (in Turkey). The king was mortally ill and had been sent an image of Jesus. St. Jude visited him and through the saint's intercession, the king was healed. (History Ecclesiastica, I, xiii.)

The image is sometimes called the Mandylion or the Mandylion of Edessa. Much has been written about miracles and tradition associated with it. There are some variations in the account, and whether it was imprinted on a medallion, or on cloth, like the Shroud of Turin.

St. Jude holding an axe or club

St. Jude was martyred for the Faith around the year 65 AD, probably in the Middle East in Syria or Persia, where he had traveled to spread the news of Jesus Christ. He was murdered along with Simon the Zealot, by decapitation with a hatchet His body was brought back to St. Peter's Basilica in Rome and buried in a vault below the church.

St. Jude holding a scroll or book

The scroll symbolizes his letter contained in the New Testament.

St. Jude holding a carpenter's rule

Perhaps St. Jude was a carpenter before becoming an apostle of Christ.

10 PRAYERS FOR EVERY DAY

OUR FATHER

Our Father, Who art in heaven,
Hallowed be Thy Name.
Thy Kingdom come.
Thy Will be done, on earth as it is in Heaven.
Give us this day our daily bread.
And forgive us our trespasses,
as we forgive those who trespass against us.
And lead us not into temptation,
but deliver us from evil. Amen.

+++

HAIL MARY

Hail Mary, Full of Grace, The Lord is with thee.
Blessed art thou among women, and blessed is the fruit
of thy womb, Jesus. Holy Mary, Mother of God,
pray for us sinners now, and at the hour of death. Amen

+++

GLORY BE

Glory be to the Father, and to the Son,
and to the Holy Spirit.
As it was in the beginning, is now, and ever shall be,
world without end. Amen

MORNING OFFERING

O Jesus, through the Immaculate Heart of Mary,

I offer You my prayers, works, joys and sufferings
of this day for all the intentions of Your Sacred Heart,
in union with the Holy Sacrifice of the Mass throughout the world,
in reparation for my sins, for the intentions of all my relatives and friends,
and in particular for the intentions of the Holy Father.
Amen.

+++

ACT OF FAITH

O my God, I firmly believe that you are one God in three divine Persons,
Father, Son, and Holy Spirit.
I believe that your divine son became man, died for our sins,
and that he will come to judge the living and the dead.
I believe these and all the truths which the holy Catholic Church teaches,
because you who have revealed them,
who can neither deceive nor be deceived. Amen.

+++

ACT OF HOPE

O my God, relying on Your almighty power and infinite mercy and promises, I hope
to obtain pardon of my sins, the help of Your grace and life everlasting, through the
merits of Jesus Christ, my Lord and Redeemer. Amen.

+++

ACT OF LOVE

O my God, I love You above all things with my whole heart and soul, because you
are all-good and worthy of all love. I love my neighbor as myself for the love of You
I forgive all who have injured me and ask pardon of all whom I have injured. Amen.

+++

ACT OF CONTRITION

O my God, I am heartily sorry for having offended Thee,
and I detest all my sins, because I dread the loss of heaven,
and the pains of hell; but most of all because they offend Thee, my God,
Who are all good and deserving of all my love.
I firmly resolve, with the help of Thy grace, to confess my sins,
to do penance, and to amend my life. Amen.

PRAYER TO MY GUARDIAN ANGEL

Angel of God, my guardian dear,
To whom God's love commits me here,
Ever this day, be at my side,
To light and guard, to rule and guide. Amen.

+++

PRAYER TO SAINT MICHAEL THE ARCHANGEL

St. Michael the Archangel, defend us in battle.
Be our protection against the wickedness and snares of the Devil.
May God rebuke him, we humbly pray, and do thou,
O Prince of the heavenly hosts, by the power of God,
cast into hell Satan, and all the evil spirits,
who prowl about the world seeking the ruin of souls. Amen..

Sitting Mary with the St. Jude Thaddeus and St. Ursula
Martin Schongauer , Date: 1475 – 1490, Style: Northern Renaissance

EPISTLE OF ST. JUDE[1]

1 Jude, the servant of Jesus Christ, and brother of James: to them that are beloved in God the Father, and preserved in Jesus Christ, and called. 2 Mercy unto you, and peace, and charity be fulfilled. 3 Dearly beloved, taking all care to write unto you concerning your common salvation, I was under a necessity to write unto you: to beseech you to contend earnestly for the faith once delivered to the saints. 4 For certain men are secretly entered in, (who were written of long ago unto this judgment,) ungodly men, turning the grace of our Lord God into riotousness, and denying the only sovereign Ruler, and our Lord Jesus Christ.

5 I will therefore admonish you, though ye once knew all things, that Jesus, having saved the people out of the land of Egypt, did afterwards destroy them that believed not: 6 And the angels who kept not their principality, but forsook their own habitation, he hath reserved under darkness in everlasting chains, unto the judgment of the great day. 7 As Sodom and Gomorrha, and the neighbouring cities, in like manner, having given themselves to fornication, and going after other flesh, were made an example, suffering the punishment of eternal fire.

8 In like manner these men also defile the flesh, and despise dominion, and blaspheme majesty. 9 When Michael the archangel, disputing with the devil, contended about the body of Moses, he durst not bring against him the judgment of railing speech, but said: The Lord command thee. 10 But these men blaspheme whatever things they know not: and what things soever they naturally know, like dumb beasts, in these they are corrupted. 11 Woe unto them, for they have gone in the way of Cain: and after the error of Balaam they have for reward poured out themselves, and have perished in the contradiction of Core. 12 These are spots in their banquets, feasting together without fear, feeding themselves, clouds without water, which are carried about by winds, trees of the autumn, unfruitful, twice dead, plucked up by the roots, 13 Raging waves of the sea, foaming out their own confusion; wandering stars, to whom the storm of darkness is reserved for ever.

[1] Douay-Rheims 1899

The Holy Bible in English, Douay-Rheims American Edition of 1899, translated from the Latin Vulgate

Translation by: English College, Douai

14 Now of these Enoch also, the seventh from Adam, prophesied, saying: Behold, the Lord cometh with thousands of his saints, 15 To execute judgment upon all, and to reprove all the ungodly for all the works of their ungodliness, whereby they have done ungodly, and of all the hard things which ungodly sinners have spoken against God. 16 These are murmurers, full of complaints, walking according to their own desires, and their mouth speaketh proud things, admiring persons for gain's sake. 17 But you, my dearly beloved, be mindful of the words which have been spoken before by the apostles of our Lord Jesus Christ, 18 Who told you, that in the last time there should come mockers, walking according to their own desires in ungodlinesses. 19 These are they who separate themselves, sensual men, having not the Spirit.

20 But you, my beloved, building yourselves upon your most holy faith, praying in the Holy Ghost, 21 Keep yourselves in the love of God, waiting for the mercy of our Lord Jesus Christ, unto life everlasting. 22 And some indeed reprove, being judged: 23 But others save, pulling them out of the fire. And on others have mercy, in fear, hating also the spotted garment which is carnal.

24 Now to him who is able to preserve you without sin, and to present you spotless before the presence of his glory with exceeding joy, in the coming of our Lord Jesus Christ, 25 To the only God our Saviour through Jesus Christ our Lord, be glory and magnificence, empire and power, before all ages, and now, and for all ages of ages. Amen.

Hans Sebald Beham, *St Jude (Thaddeus)*,
plate 10 from the suite The Twelve Apostles, ca. 1546,
engraving on paper, Museum Purchase: Vivian and Gordon Gilkey Endowment Fund,
public domain, 1999.70.2j

Printed in Great Britain
by Amazon